MW01599152

Profiles of the Presidents

FRANKLIN D. ROOSEVELT

★ ★ ★

Profiles of the Presidents

FRANKLIN D. ROOSEVELT

by Michael Burgan

Content Adviser: Harry Rubenstein, Curator of Political History Collections, National Museum of American History, Smithsonian Institution
Social Science Adviser: Professor Sherry L. Field, Department of Curriculum and Instruction, College of Education, The University of Texas at Austin
Reading Adviser: Dr. Linda D. Labbo, Department of Reading Education, College of Education, The University of Georgia

COMPASS POINT BOOKS ✦ MINNEAPOLIS, MINNESOTA

Compass Point Books
3722 West 50th Street, #115
Minneapolis, MN 55410

Visit Compass Point Books on the Internet at *www.compasspointbooks.com*
or e-mail your request to *custserv@compasspointbooks.com*

Editors: E. Russell Primm, Emily J. Dolbear, and Melissa McDaniel
Photo Researchers: Svetlana Zhurkina and Jo Miller
Photo Selector: Catherine Neitge
Designer: The Design Lab

Library of Congress Cataloging-in-Publication Data

Burgan, Michael.
   Franklin D. Roosevelt / by Michael Burgan.
     p. cm. — (Profiles of the presidents)
   Includes bibliographical references and index.
   Summary: A biography of the wheelchair-bound president who optimistically led the United States through more than a decade of economic, social, and political problems.
   ISBN 0-7565-0203-9
   1. Roosevelt, Franklin D. (Franklin Delano), 1882–1945—Juvenile literature. 2. Presidents—United States—Biography—Juvenile literature. [1. Roosevelt, Franklin D. (Franklin Delano), 1882–1945. 2.Presidents.] I. Title. II. Series.
   E807 .B833 2002
   973.917'092—dc21   2001004736

Table of Contents

★ ★ ★

A President with Hope

★ ★ ★

From 1933 to 1945, the United States faced some of the darkest years in its history. First, the economy collapsed. Millions of people were forced out of work and into poverty. This is now known as the Great Depression. Then World War II (1939–1945) threatened the freedom of America's **allies**—and possibly America's freedom, too.

During those troubled times, America had just one president—Franklin D. Roosevelt. FDR, as he was called, had many qualities of a good leader. He chose talented people to help him run the government. He was willing to try new ideas to solve America's problems. Perhaps most importantly, he had courage and a good attitude. He was able to convince Americans that they could survive the Great Depression and win World War II.

Roosevelt had endured serious troubles in his life. At age thirty-nine, he contracted a disease called **polio.**

The disease crippled him and forced him to use a wheelchair for the rest of his life.

He also made many enemies during his career. His policies upset some people. They thought he was going to take away their wealth and ruin the nation. Other Americans thought he did not do enough to help workers, African-Americans, and the poor. But Roosevelt rarely backed down from the people who challenged him.

Throughout his presidency, he received great support from his wife, Eleanor. Like her husband, Eleanor had a

◄ *Franklin Delano Roosevelt gives the V-for-victory sign.*

Eleanor and Franklin Roosevelt in 1938 ▲

strong personality. Both Roosevelts devoted their lives to serving the people.

Roosevelt's policies helped change American government. He believed that the government sometimes needs to play a more active role in solving problems. Today, Americans still argue about how large that role should be.

Childhood Riches

★ ★ ★

During the late nineteenth century, businessmen such as Cornelius Vanderbilt and John Rockefeller made huge fortunes. But the average worker barely made two dollars a day.

Roosevelt's family home in Hyde Park ▾

The Vanderbilts had a home near the Roosevelt family's home in Hyde Park, New York. The Roosevelts were not as rich as the Vanderbilts—but they were much wealthier than most Americans of that time.

Franklin was born on January 30, 1882,

Franklin with
his mother,
Sara, in 1887

the only child of James and Sara Roosevelt. (His father had another son from an earlier marriage.) Sara's family, the Delano family, was also wealthy. As a child, Franklin often traveled to Europe with his parents. Until he became a teenager, he studied at home. For fun, his father taught him how to fish and sail. Franklin loved the water throughout his life.

In 1896, Franklin left home to study at Groton, a private boys' school in Massachusetts. The head of the school, Endicott Peabody, urged his students to help others, especially the poor. Peabody's ideas became very important to Franklin.

Another important person in Franklin's life was his

fifth cousin Theodore. "Teddy" Roosevelt won fame in 1898 as a soldier during the Spanish-American War. At that time, Franklin was still in high school. In 1900, when Franklin was at Harvard University, his cousin was elected vice president of the United States. Normally, Franklin supported the Democratic Party, as his father did. But Franklin was happy to back his cousin, who was a Republican.

▲ *Franklin with his father, James, and mother, Sara, in 1903*

The next year, President William McKinley was **assassinated** and suddenly Teddy Roosevelt was president. Teddy, also known as TR, had strong views. He believed

President Theodore Roosevelt

that the government should help shape the economy and improve people's lives. He also wanted the United States to become active in world politics. In many ways, Teddy's beliefs shaped Franklin's political ideas.

In 1902, Franklin grew close to another relative—his distant cousin and Teddy's niece, Eleanor Roosevelt. Like Franklin, Eleanor wanted to help the poor. She once took

◄ *Eleanor and Franklin Roosevelt in 1908 with Anna and baby James*

Franklin to New York to show him the dreadful poverty in America's cities.

In 1905, Franklin and Eleanor married. During the next eleven years, they had one daughter and five sons (one son died when he was a child). Franklin and Eleanor did not have a perfect marriage, but they stayed together despite their problems. They also worked together on their shared goals of helping others and leading the United States through difficult times.

Stepping into Politics

★ ★ ★

After graduating from Harvard, Roosevelt studied law in New York and became a lawyer. TR—"Uncle Ted"—told Franklin that he should go into politics. In 1910, FDR took his advice. He won a seat in the New York state senate.

Roosevelt wanted New York to have a better government. At that time, powerful men called "bosses" controlled politics in New York. These political bosses decided who would work in government. They decided how to spend government money.

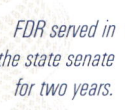
FDR served in the state senate for two years.

Roosevelt was taking on powerful people to try to improve the government. He told a reporter, "There is nothing I love as much as a good fight."

▲ *Franklin Roosevelt, far left, at the Brooklyn Navy Yard in 1914*

Roosevelt served in the New York senate for two years. Then, in 1913, he took a huge step forward in his political career. He was named assistant **secretary** of the U.S. Navy. As assistant secretary, Roosevelt wanted the navy to grow and become more modern. The United States **fleet** was smaller than those of Great Britain and

Franklin, Eleanor, and their family in 1919

Germany. When World War I (1914–1918) began in Europe, Roosevelt knew the United States had to be ready. After America entered the war in 1917, Roosevelt visited battlefields in Europe. Years later, Roosevelt told a crowd, "I have seen war. . . . I have seen the dead in the mud. I have seen cities destroyed. . . . I hate war."

In 1920, after the war ended, Roosevelt left his navy job. By then, he was well known. That summer, the Democratic Party chose Roosevelt to run for vice president.

Roosevelt called his selection "the greatest possible surprise." He also joked that it "upset my plans for a peaceful summer!"

Roosevelt and James Cox, the Democratic **candidate** for president, traveled across the country making speeches and trying to win votes. Roosevelt sometimes gave seven speeches a day. Despite this hard work, the Democrats lost.

▲ *FDR, right, and James Cox campaigned in Dayton, Ohio, in 1920.*

Roosevelt returned to New York, formed his own law firm, and entered the business world. He planned to return to politics someday. But suddenly, he was struck by a serious illness—one that would almost end his career.

In August 1921, Roosevelt was on vacation on Campobello Island, off New Brunswick, Canada. During the stay, his legs started feeling strange. It became hard to

Roosevelt waved to supporters in 1920, the year before he learned he had polio.

move them. Two weeks later, a doctor told Roosevelt that he had polio. This disease is rare in the United States today, but it was common in the 1920s. Polio can **paralyze,** or cripple, a person's legs.

The doctors told Roosevelt that he had a mild case of polio. They thought he would get better. Roosevelt himself believed that he would walk again one day. They were wrong. For the rest of his life, Roosevelt walked with crutches or used a wheelchair. Still, he was set on overcoming his disability. He exercised every day to make his upper body stronger and to relax his legs. He learned how to drive a car using handles instead of pedals. He kept traveling and giving speeches. Roosevelt also helped many other people who had polio.

FDR with a young girl at his Hyde Park, New York, home

In 1927, he started a center in Warm Springs, Georgia, where people with polio could be treated.

At first, Roosevelt was bitter about his disease. He had always been active in sports, and he had high goals for his career. But, over time, his hardship helped make him a stronger person. Eleanor later wrote, "He soon discovered that the way to lighten all **burdens** is to take them cheerfully." That discovery, Eleanor believed, taught Roosevelt how to cheer up others during hard times.

The Great Depression

★ ★ ★

In 1928, Roosevelt returned to politics and was elected governor of New York. Once again, he fought for many changes. He tried to improve the courts and jails. He supported lower prices for electricity, and he also started programs to help farmers earn more money for their crops.

During most of the 1920s, the U.S. economy boomed. The era is sometimes called the Roaring Twenties. Workers were earning higher wages. They gladly spent their money on cars and other new products, such as

Roosevelt was ▶ elected governor of New York in 1928.

◄ As the economy boomed, people could afford to buy cars, such as this 1920 Ford Runabout.

radios and refrigerators. Many Americans also invested in the stock market. They bought shares in companies. Over time, the value of these shares grew.

Many farmers, however, faced tough times during the 1920s. Food prices fell, but the farmers kept growing crops and raising livestock. Many farmers could not live on the small amount of money they earned. By 1929, the farm problems made it clear that America's economy was not as strong as it seemed.

The real end of the economic boom began on Thursday, October 24—a day that came to be called Black Thursday. The price of stocks started to fall. People rushed to sell their stocks before the prices dropped even

HERBERT HOOVER
FOR PRESIDENT

Crowds ran through Wall Street following news of the stock market crash.

President Herbert Hoover

further. On the following Tuesday, October 29—later known as Black Tuesday—the stock market lost $14 billion in value. Many people lost all their money. Black Thursday was the start of the Great Depression.

President Herbert Hoover told Americans that these troubles would soon end—but times only got harder. More companies closed. More workers lost their jobs. More parents struggled to find food for their hungry children. And, like many other leaders of the Republican Party, President Hoover did not think that the government could do anything to help.

◀ *Some families who lost everything during the Great Depression lived in shantytowns called Hoovervilles, such as this one in Washington, D.C.*

FDR thought differently. He believed it was the government's duty to help Americans who were suffering during the Great Depression.

Finally, President Hoover decided that the government should help after all. He took some steps to end the Great Depression, but they were too little and too late. He still did not believe that the government should give money to the unemployed and to the poor. By 1932, however, more Americans shared Roosevelt's ideas about the role of the government. In July, the Democratic Party chose FDR to run for president against Hoover. John N. Garner was the Democratic vice presidential candidate.

A New Deal

★ ★ ★

At the Democratic **convention,** Roosevelt gave one of his most famous speeches. He attacked the Republican Party, saying, "In disaster, they have held out no hope." Roosevelt also made a promise: "I pledge you—I pledge myself to a new deal for the American people." From then on,

FDR waves to the ▶
crowd in 1932.

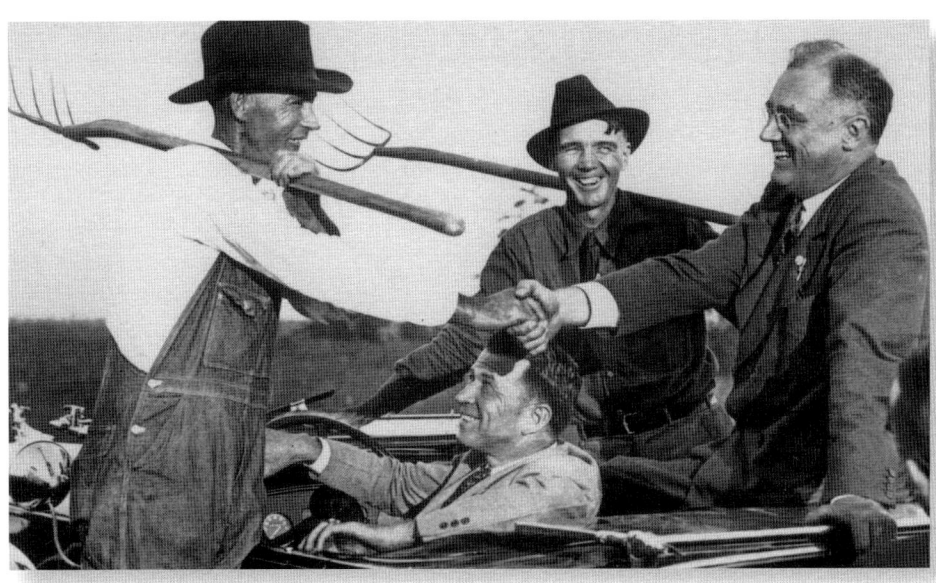

◀ *Roosevelt talks with two Georgia farmers in 1932.*

Roosevelt talked about how, in his "new deal," the government would use its power to end the Great Depression.

Roosevelt often spoke about trying to help average Americans instead of aiding large businesses. He had many of the same ideas as his cousin Teddy. FDR was willing to go even further than his cousin did, however. He had to. The nation was facing deep problems and they were getting worse.

In November 1932, Roosevelt won the election easily. He was a natural leader. He had a strong personality, a good sense of humor, and a winning smile. He loved talking to people and making speeches. He always seemed calm and sure of himself. People trusted him.

Franklin D. Roosevelt takes the oath of office as the thirty-second president on March 4, 1933.

Roosevelt did not take office until March 4, 1933. By then, the nation's economy had grown worse. Many banks failed, as people rushed to take all their money out. In his first speech as president of the United States, Roosevelt set the tone for how he would approach the country's problems. He said he had a "firm belief that the only thing we have to fear is fear itself." After he was sworn in, the president quickly went to work.

The next day he ordered all the banks in the country

to close for four days. That way people would not be able to take out their money and possibly cause more banks to fail. Soon, Congress passed the Emergency Banking Relief Act to help the banks. Later, it created the Federal Deposit Insurance Corporation. This new agency guaranteed that people would

▲ *Secretary of the Treasury William Woodin watches as FDR signs the emergency banking bill in March 1933.*

get their money back even if a bank failed. The rush to pull money out of the banks ended.

Roosevelt also started many new government programs and agencies. The Tennessee Valley Authority helped to build dams and power plants that made energy for people in seven states. The Agricultural Adjustment Act helped support farmers. The Civilian Conservation Corps put 2.5 million young people to work in the nation's parks and forests.

The National Industrial Recovery Act helped many

Workers at a Civilian ▸
Conservation Corps
construction camp in
California in 1933

workers. It set a limit on the number of hours people could work each week and made sure they were paid fairly for their work. It also allowed workers to form **labor unions**—organizations that represented workers to convince business owners to improve wages and working conditions.

This first, busy part of Roosevelt's presidency was later called the First Hundred Days. Roosevelt wanted to show that he was ready to tackle the problems of the Great Depression. Even some Republicans admired his style. One senator wrote that Roosevelt "has the guts to try. . . . Where there was hesitation . . . there is now courage and boldness and real action."

Although Roosevelt knew what he wanted to accomplish, he wasn't always sure how to do it. To help him decide, he relied on his advisers. Some of his advisers were the heads of important government agencies. Together, they are called the president's cabinet. One of FDR's cabinet members was Frances Perkins, the secretary of labor. She was the first woman to serve in a presidential cabinet. Another important adviser to Roosevelt was his wife, Eleanor.

Despite the new programs, the U.S. economy still struggled. In the summer of 1935, Roosevelt and Congress created more programs to fight the Great Depression.

During this time, Roosevelt created the Works Progress Administration (WPA). Over the next few

Roosevelt with Frances Perkins, the first woman to serve in the cabinet

29

years, this program put more than 8 million Americans to work building roads, bridges, parks, and airports. The WPA also created jobs for millions of writers, artists, and actors.

Another one of FDR's new programs was Social Security. This program gave money to the jobless, the elderly, and the disabled. Social Security is still active today.

Roosevelt was the first president to use the radio to successfully communicate with the American people. His informal radio speeches called fireside chats raised the spir-

FDR's "fireside chats" on the radio helped lift the spirits of Americans.

◀ *A huge dust storm approaches the village of Rolla, Kansas, in the mid-1930s.*

its of the troubled country. Listening to Roosevelt in their homes, millions of Americans felt he was speaking directly to them. In his fireside chats, he calmly and carefully explained his New Deal. On the whole, Americans agreed with his policies. In 1936, Roosevelt easily won reelection.

Many Americans, however, still had problems. In the Great Plains, a terrible **drought** killed crops, and many farmers were forced to leave their land. African-Americans and other minorities also suffered. They had a harder time finding jobs than white Americans did and they often had to live in poor housing. Although many blacks supported Roosevelt, they did not always get their fair share of help from the New Deal.

Factory workers also struggled. Those lucky enough to have jobs sometimes fought with their employers. Workers formed labor unions to demand better wages and working conditions, but business owners often did not agree to these demands. Many workers then went on **strike,** refusing to work. These strikes sometimes led to violence.

Roosevelt's policies could not solve all these problems. His ideas also created enemies. Some business owners and rich people accused FDR of wanting **socialism.** Under socialism, the government owns most businesses. Roosevelt insisted that he supported the U.S. system in which private citizens own the businesses. But he added, "'freedom' and 'opportunity' do not mean a license to climb upwards by pushing other people down."

Republicans worried that the government was becoming too powerful in the business world. They also did not believe that the government should give money to unemployed people. In 1935, the Supreme Court of the United States had overturned the National Recovery Act. The justices said that the president did not have the right to be so involved in the country's economy.

FDR was angry that the Supreme Court did not support him. He wanted to increase the number of justices on the court. He wanted to name new justices who would

◀ *The Supreme Court did not support some of FDR's programs.*

This photo by Dorothea Lange of a poor migrant mother and her children came to symbolize the Great Depression for many Americans.

back his programs. Many Americans were against his plan, however, and the president lost congressional support for the plan.

Another problem came later that year. The president's new programs had cost billions of dollars. Roosevelt thought they were working so well that it would be safe to cut government spending. But his budget cuts hurt the economy. By March 1938, another 4 million people were out of work. Congress quickly called for new spending to help.

The next year, more than 9 million Americans were still out of work. The New Deal programs had helped, but they were not able to stop the Great Depression. Events outside the United States finally ended the depression—but at a high cost.

World at War

★ ★ ★

The Great Depression was a problem all over the world. People in many nations were jobless and hungry. Other countries also had political problems. Adolf Hitler and his Nazi Party ruled Germany. Hitler used violence to stay in power. Other nations, such as Italy and Japan, also had governments that ruled harshly.

Roosevelt watched world events carefully. In Germany, Hitler was building up his military forces. Japan had already taken over

Adolf Hitler at a Nazi rally

Roosevelt onboard an American warship in the mid-1930s ▲ parts of China and wanted to control more of its neighbors' land.

Roosevelt believed the United States had to help stop the spread of this violence. Most Americans, however, did not want the country to get involved in other nations' problems.

By 1939, many people believed a great war would soon begin in Europe. Germany had taken control of Austria and Czechoslovakia, and German troops were ready to invade more countries. On September 1, 1939, the Germans made a surprise attack on Poland. Great

Britain and France—Poland's allies—then went to war against Germany and its ally, Italy. World War II had begun.

Great Britain and France had hoped that the Soviet Union would help them fight Germany and Italy. They did not know that the Soviet Union had already signed a secret agreement with Germany. The Soviet Union and Germany had agreed not to go to war with each other.

▲ A Czech woman cried as she gave the Nazi salute after her country was seized by the Germans in 1938.

Roosevelt told Americans that the United States would not take sides in the war. The president, however, wanted to help Great Britain and France, so he convinced Congress to sell them weapons. The need for planes and other supplies created new jobs for Americans. As the war grew, so did the number of jobs. These new jobs finally led to the end of the Great Depression.

As the depression was ending, the United States was

German troops ▶ marched near the Arc de Triomphe after the fall of Paris in 1940.

drawing closer to war. Roosevelt asked Congress to build more weapons for U.S. forces, just in case the country had to enter the war.

That seemed more likely as time went on. In June 1940, Hitler's forces rolled through France. They had already taken Belgium, Norway, Denmark, and the Netherlands. Later in the summer, German planes began bombing Great Britain.

That year, Roosevelt ran for president a third time. No U.S. president had ever served three terms. In this election, the Republican candidate was Wendell L. Willkie. He told Americans that it was dangerous for one man to remain president for too long. He said that Roosevelt would have too much power and would lead the nation into war.

But Roosevelt wanted to stay in office to help Great Britain and France. He wanted to finish what he had started. In November 1940, he was elected president for the third time.

A few weeks after his election, Roosevelt warned Americans that the country faced its greatest danger ever. Japan had joined with Germany and Italy in the war. These three countries were called the Axis Powers. Great Britain and France were called the Allied Powers, or Allies. If the Axis Powers defeated the Allies, Roosevelt said, "all of us in all the Americas would be living at the point of a gun—a gun loaded with explosive bullets, economic as well as military."

Later, Roosevelt told Americans that

A portrait of Franklin D. Roosevelt from the White House collection

The USS Arizona *burning after the Japanese attack on Pearl Harbor*

the United States believed in protecting four basic freedoms throughout the world. These were freedom of speech, freedom of religion, freedom from want (poverty), and freedom from fear. The president was preparing the country for war. It finally came on December 7, 1941.

At the port of Pearl Harbor, in Hawaii, U.S. Navy ships sat tied to their docks on a quiet Sunday morning. Without warning, hundreds of Japanese planes attacked Pearl Harbor. In two hours, the Japanese sank 12 U.S. ships and killed nearly 2,400 Americans.

The next day, the United States declared war against Japan. Within a few days, the United States was also at war with Germany and Italy.

In 1941, Germany had broken its agreement with the Soviet Union by invading it. The Soviet Union then joined the Allied forces in the war. The United States became one of the Allied forces. As World War II went on, Roosevelt met several times with the other Allied leaders—Joseph Stalin, the leader of the Soviet Union, and Winston Churchill, the prime minister of Great Britain. These three men were known as the Big Three.

While the U.S. military fought the war, Roosevelt worked on the home front. Once again, he tried to give

▲ FDR signing the declaration of war against Germany and Italy

Americans hope in his fireside chats. He also focused the American economy on the war effort. Wages and prices were controlled by the government. Unions promised not to go on strike. The government set limits on how much gas and other goods people could buy. "The price for **civilization**," Roosevelt said, "must be paid in hard work and sorrow and blood."

Roosevelt also worked with other nations involved in the war. On January 1, 1942, leaders from twenty-six nations that were fighting the Axis forces met at the

The Big Three: ▶
Joseph Stalin, left,
Franklin Roosevelt,
and Winston
Churchill

White House. They agreed to work together to win the war. Roosevelt referred to them as the "United Nations." During the war, he began to plan an organization called the United Nations that would work to prevent future wars. Today's United Nations is the result of his work.

By 1944, the Allies were starting to win the war. Italy had given up, and the Soviet Union was slowly pushing back the German army. In Western Europe, the Allies were planning to invade France.

▲ *President Roosevelt looks at a map during his nationwide tour of war plants and military training centers in 1943.*

Democrats again chose FDR as their candidate for president in 1944.

Roosevelt was also thinking about running for a fourth term as president. "I don't want to," he said, "but I may find it necessary." Again, Roosevelt wanted to finish what he had started. He wanted to make sure the Allies

won the war. He also wanted to be sure that the United States could keep the peace once the fighting stopped.

▲ Harry Truman and Franklin Roosevelt

Once again, Roosevelt was reelected. His vice president was Harry S. Truman. Roosevelt was the first and last U.S. president ever to be elected to four terms. The laws were later changed so that U.S. presidents may be elected to only two terms.

By early 1945, the end of the war seemed near. The invasion of France, called D-Day, had been a great victory

The Big Three of Winston Churchill, left, Franklin Roosevelt, and Joseph Stalin met in Yalta in 1945.

for the Allies. The United States was also fighting well in the Pacific.

Roosevelt, however, had personal problems. His health was beginning to fail. In February, the Big Three met in Yalta in the Soviet Union to talk about how to handle Germany after the war. Roosevelt did not look well during that meeting.

Although the United States and the Soviet Union worked together during the war, they did not completely trust each other. Roosevelt tried to get along with Stalin. He sometimes told jokes and called him "Uncle Joe." A few weeks after Yalta, however, the president said, "We can't do business with Stalin. He has broken every one of his promises." Roosevelt sensed that problems could develop between the United States and the Soviet Union. He was afraid that the Soviet leader would try to block his plans for the United Nations.

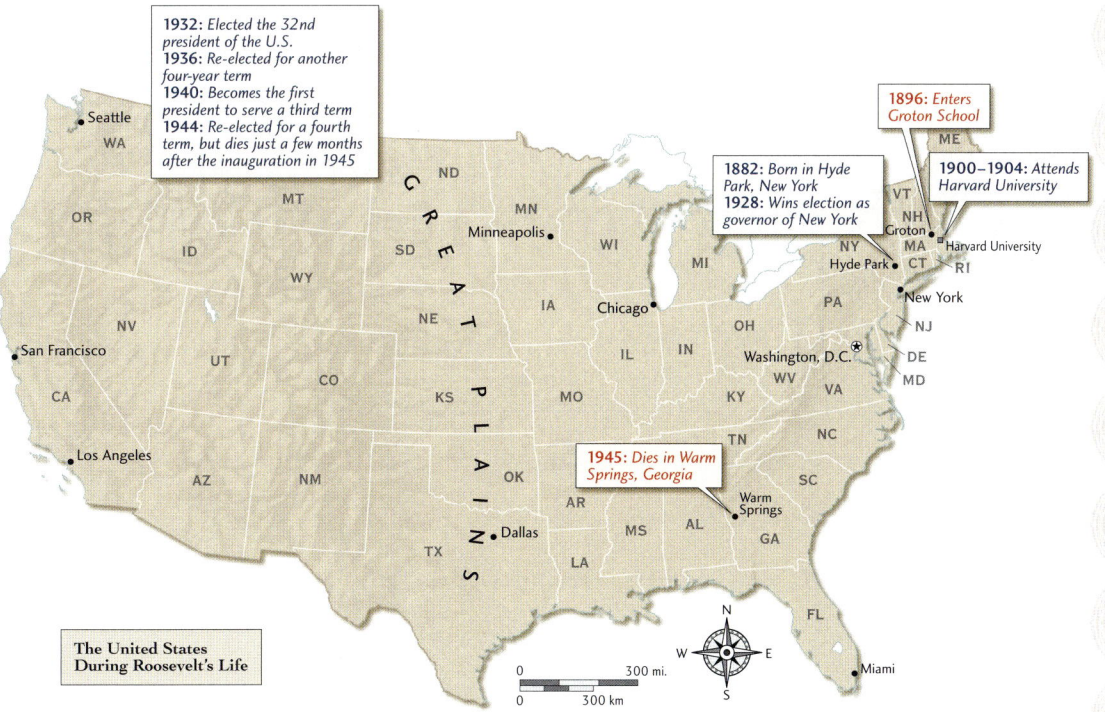

1932: Elected the 32nd president of the U.S.
1936: Re-elected for another four-year term
1940: Becomes the first president to serve a third term
1944: Re-elected for a fourth term, but dies just a few months after the inauguration in 1945

1896: Enters Groton School

1882: Born in Hyde Park, New York
1928: Wins election as governor of New York

1900–1904: Attends Harvard University

1945: Dies in Warm Springs, Georgia

The United States During Roosevelt's Life

Making a Difference

★ ★ ★

Roosevelt never learned what happened between the United States and the Soviet Union. He never saw the Allied victory over the Axis forces that August. On April 12, 1945, while vacationing in Warm Springs, Georgia, the president suddenly got a terrible headache. A few hours later, he was dead.

Roosevelt's death stunned the nation. Winston Churchill, who had worked closely with FDR throughout the war, also felt the loss. "One day," Churchill told an American reporter, "the world, and history, will know what it owes to your president."

Roosevelt served in office longer than any other U.S. president. During those years, he changed the role of the president. He also changed the role of the government in people's lives. After having FDR in the White House, many Americans expected the president to be a leader on many

A newsboy sells papers with the news of Roosevelt's death on April 12, 1945.

THEY (WHO) SEEK TO ESTABLISH SYSTEMS OF GOVERNMENT BASED ON THE REGIMENTATION OF ALL HUMAN BEINGS BY A HANDFUL OF INDIVIDUAL RULERS... CALL THIS A NEW ORDER. IT IS NOT NEW AND IT IS NOT ORDER

▲ *Statues of FDR and his dog, Fala, are part of the Franklin Delano Roosevelt Memorial on the Mall in Washington, D.C.*

issues, especially the economy. Many also expected the government to help fight poverty and other social problems.

Like any president, Roosevelt had flaws. But he was a strong leader. He gave Americans hope and kept them united through some of the most difficult times this country has faced. Even on the day he died, Roosevelt shared with Americans—once again—his great courage and his hopeful spirit: "Let us move forward," he wrote, "with strong and active faith."

GLOSSARY

allies—countries that support one another in a conflict

assassinated—to murder someone who is well known or important

burdens—serious responsibilities

candidate—someone running for office in an election

civilization—a highly developed society

convention—a large meeting during which a political party chooses its candidates

drought—a long spell of very dry weather

fleet—a number of ships under one command

labor unions—organizations formed to improve workers' wages and working conditions

paralyze—to make someone or something unable to move

polio—short form of the word poliomyelitis, a disease that may cause paralysis

secretary—the head of a government department

socialism—an economic system in which the government owns most businesses

strike—when workers refuse to work, hoping to force their employer to agree to their demands

FRANLIN D. ROOSEVELT'S LIFE AT A GLANCE

★ ★ ★

PERSONAL

Nickname:	FDR
Born:	January 30, 1882
Birthplace:	Hyde Park, New York
Father's name:	James Roosevelt
Mother's name:	Sara Delano Roosevelt
Education:	Graduated Harvard College (1903), Columbia Law School (1907)
Wife's name:	Anna Eleanor Roosevelt
Married:	March 17, 1905
Children:	Anna Eleanor Roosevelt (1906–1975); James Roosevelt (1907–1991); Franklin Delano Roosevelt Jr. (died in infancy, 1909); Elliott Roosevelt (1910–1990); Franklin Delano Roosevelt Jr. (1914–1988); John Aspinwall Roosevelt (1916–1981)
Died:	April 12, 1945, in Warm Springs, Georgia
Buried:	Hyde Park, New York

*Franklin D. Roosevelt's
Life at a Glance*

PUBLIC

Occupation before presidency: Lawyer, public official

Occupation after presidency: None

Military service: None

Other government positions: New York state senator, assistant secretary of the navy, governor of New York

Political party: Democrat

Vice presidents: John N. Garner (1933–1941)
Henry A. Wallace (1941–1945)
Harry S. Truman (1945)

Dates in office: March 4, 1933–April 12, 1945

Presidential opponents: President Herbert Hoover (Republican), 1932; Governor Alfred M. Landon (Republican), 1936; Wendell L. Willkie (Republican), 1940; Governor Thomas E. Dewey (Republican), 1944

Number of votes (Electoral College): 22,825,016 of 38,583,413 (472 of 531), 1932; 27,747,636 of 44,427,179 (523 of 531), 1936; 27,263,448 of 49,799,708 (449 of 531), 1940; 25,611,936 of 47,625,308 (432 of 531), 1944

Writings: *The Happy Warrior, Alfred E. Smith* (1928); *F.D.R.: His Personal Letters* (4 vols., 1947–1950), ed. by Elliott Roosevelt

Franklin D. Roosevelt's Cabinet

Secretary of state:
Cordell Hull (1933–1944)
Edward R. Stettinius Jr. (1944–1945)

Secretary of the treasury:
William H. Woodin (1933–1934)
Henry Morgenthau Jr. (1934–1945)

Secretary of war:
George H. Dern (1933–1936)
Harry H. Woodring (1937–1940)
Henry L. Stimson (1940–1945)

Attorney general:
Homer S. Cummings (1933–1939)
Frank Murphy (1939–1940)
Robert H. Jackson (1940–1941)
Francis B. Biddle (1941–1945)

Postmaster general:
James A. Farley (1933–1940)
Frank C. Walker (1940–1945)

Secretary of the navy:
Claude A. Swanson (1933–1939)
Charles Edison (1940)
Frank Knox (1940–1944)
James V. Forrestal (1944–1945)

Secretary of the interior:
Harold L. Ickes (1933–1945)

Secretary of agriculture:
Henry A. Wallace (1933–1940)
Claude R. Wickard (1940–1945)

Secretary of commerce:
Daniel C. Roper (1933–1938)
Harry L. Hopkins (1938–1940)
Jesse H. Jones (1940–1945)
Henry A. Wallace (1945)

Secretary of labor:
Frances Perkins (1933–1945)

FRANKLIN D. ROOSEVELT'S LIFE AND TIMES

★ ★ ★

ROOSEVELT'S LIFE

January 30, Roosevelt is born in Hyde Park, New York (below) — 1882

Attends Groton, a famed Massachusetts prep school — 1896–1900

WORLD EVENTS

1882 — Thomas Edison builds a power station

1884 — Mark Twain publishes *The Adventures of Huckleberry Finn*

1886 — Grover Cleveland dedicates the Statue of Liberty in New York

Bombing in Haymarket Square, Chicago, due to labor unrest

1890

1891 — The Roman Catholic Church publishes the encyclical *Rerum Novarum,* which supports the rights of labor

1893 — Women gain voting privileges in New Zealand, the first country to take such a step

1896 — The Olympic Games are held for the first time in recent history, in Athens, Greece

ROOSEVELT'S LIFE

WORLD EVENTS

1900

1910

Year	Roosevelt's Life	Year	World Events
		1899	Isadora Duncan, one of the founders of modern dance, makes her debut in Chicago
1903	Graduates from Harvard University, receiving a B.A. in history	1903	Brothers Orville and Wilbur Wright successfully fly a powered airplane (below)
1905	Marries Anna Eleanor Roosevelt		
1907	Graduates from Columbia Law School		
		1909	The National Association for the Advancement of Colored People (NAACP) is founded
1910	Enters politics as a Democrat in the New York senate		
1913–1920	Serves as assistant secretary of the navy (below)	1913	Henry Ford begins to use standard assembly lines to produce automobiles
		1914	Archduke Francis Ferdinand is assassinated, launching World War I (1914–1918)
		1916	German-born physicist Albert Einstein publishes his general theory of relativity

ROOSEVELT'S LIFE

Runs for vice president (above) on the Democratic ticket, but loses — 1920

1920

Serves as governor of New York (above) — 1928–1932

WORLD EVENTS

1917 — Vladimir Ilyich Lenin and Leon Trotsky lead Bolsheviks in a rebellion against the czars in Russia during the October Revolution

1919 — World War I peace conference begins at Versailles, France

1920 — American women get the right to vote

1922 — James Joyce publishes *Ulysses*

The tomb of Tutankhamen is discovered by British archaeologist Howard Carter

1923 — French actress Sarah Bernhardt dies

1926 — A. A. Milne publishes *Winnie the Pooh*

Claude Monet and Mary Cassat, well-known impressionist painters, die

1928 — Penicillin, the first antibiotic, is discovered by Scottish scientist Alexander Fleming

1929 — The stock exchange collapses (left) and severe economic depression sets in

ROOSEVELT'S LIFE

1932 Wins the Democratic nomination for president

1933 February 15, Giuseppe Zangara attempts to kill Roosevelt

March 5, orders all the nation's banks closed on March 6 for four days

March 9–June 16, During the so-called Hundred Days, New Deal programs are passed, including the Agricultural Adjustment Act (AAA), the Tennessee Valley Authority Act, and the National Industrial Recovery Act (NIRA)

March 12, delivers his first "fireside chat" (below)

1933–1942 The Civilian Conservation Corps (right) gives jobs to 2.5 million people

1934 In July, travels to South America, becoming the first U.S. president to do so

WORLD EVENTS

1930

1930 Designs for the first jet engine are submitted to the Patent Office in Britain

1933 Nazi leader Adolf Hitler (right) is named chancellor of Germany

Presidential Election Results:		*Popular Votes*	*Electoral Votes*
1932	Franklin D. Roosevelt	22,825,016	472
	Herbert C. Hoover	15,758,397	59
1936	Franklin D. Roosevelt	27,747,636	523
	Alfred M. Landon	16,679,543	8
1940	Franklin D. Roosevelt	27,263,448	449
	Wendell L. Willkie	22,336,260	82
1944	Franklin D. Roosevelt	25,611,936	432
	Thomas E. Dewey	22,013,372	99

ROOSEVELT'S LIFE

WORLD EVENTS

The United States signs trade agreements with Brazil, Colombia, Costa Rica, Cuba, El Salvador, Guatemala, Haiti, Honduras, Nicaragua, and Canada	1934–1937		
The Social Security Act is passed (left)	1935	1935	George Gershwin's *Porgy and Bess* opera opens in New York
The Works Progress Administration (WPA) is started (left)			
The Supreme Court strikes down the NIRA, the AAA, the Railroad Retirement Act, and other New Deal programs			
Attempts to increase the number of justices on the Supreme Court fail	1937		
September 1, Germany invades Poland, starting World War II	1939	1939	German troops (above) invade Poland. Britain and France declare war on Germany. World War II (1939–45) begins.
The United States agrees to sell weapons to any nations fighting the Axis forces if they pay in cash and provide their own transportation			Hollywood produces the film version of *Gone with the Wind*
			Commercial television is introduced to America
			The film *The Wizard of Oz* is released

ROOSEVELT'S LIFE

In June, France
surrenders to Germany

1940

January 6, declares the
Four Freedoms—
freedom of speech,
freedom of worship,
freedom from want,
freedom from fear

1941

In July, the United States
limits exports to Japan

December 8, the U.S.
Congress declares war on
Japan

December 11, Germany
and Italy declare war on
the United States

November 8, the Allies
invade North Africa

1942

February 11, attends the
Yalta Conference with
Joseph Stalin and
Winston Churchill
(above)

1945

April 12, dies while still
president

WORLD EVENTS

1941   December 7, Japanese
bombers attack Pearl
Harbor, Hawaii (below),
and America enters
World War II

1942   Japanese Americans are
placed in internment
camps due to fear of
disloyalty

1944   DNA (deoxyribonucleic
acid) is found to be the
basis of heredity

1945   America drops atomic
bombs on the Japanese
cities of Hiroshima
and Nagasaki to end
World War II

The United Nations
is founded

1940

59

UNDERSTANDING FRANKLIN D. ROOSEVELT AND HIS PRESIDENCY

★ ★ ★

IN THE LIBRARY

Adams, Simon. *World War II.* New York: Dorling Kindersley, 2000.

Burgan, Michael. *The Great Depression.* Minneapolis: Compass Point Books, 2001.

Isaacs, Sally Senzell. *America at the Time of Franklin Delano Roosevelt, 1929–1948.* Chicago: Heinemann Library, 2000.

Spies, Karen Bornemann. *Franklin D. Roosevelt.* Springfield, N.J.: Enslow Publishers, 1999.

ON THE WEB

Roosevelt's Presidency
http://www.americanpresident.org/KoTrain/Courses/FDR/FDR_In_Brief.htm
For a biography of FDR by the Public Broadcasting System and links to some of his speeches

Franklin D. Roosevelt Library and Digital Archives
http://www.fdrlibrary.marist.edu
For online versions of some of the research material kept at the FDR Library and Museum

Internet Public Library—Franklin D. Roosevelt
http://www.ipl.org/ref/POTUS/fdroosevelt.html
For information and links on every U.S. president

ROOSEVELT HISTORIC SITES ACROSS THE COUNTRY

Franklin Delano Roosevelt Memorial
West Basin Drive—Tidal Basin
Washington, DC
202/426-6841
202/228-2491
To see the memorial to FDR including four outdoor "rooms," one for each of Roosevelt's four terms as president.

Franklin Delano Roosevelt Presidential Library and Museum
4079 Albany Post Road
Hyde Park, NY
845/229-8114
To visit the first presidential library. It was created by Roosevelt himself and is the only presidential library to be used by a sitting president.

The Home of Franklin Delano Roosevelt
4079 Albany Post Road
Hyde Park, NY
845/229-9115
To see the Roosevelt family estate where FDR grew up and later lived with his wife

Roosevelt Campobello International Park
459 Route 774
Welshpool, Campobello
New Brunswick, Canada
506/752-2922
To see the cottage and grounds where Roosevelt and his family vacationed during the summer. The park is on an island that Canada and the United States share.

Little White House State Historic Site
401 Little White House Road
Georgia Highway 85 Alt
Warm Springs, GA
706/655-5870
To see the home where Roosevelt went to recover from polio. It is also the site where he died.

THE U.S. PRESIDENTS
(Years in Office)

★ ★ ★

1. George Washington
   (March 4, 1789–March 3, 1797)
2. John Adams
   (March 4, 1797–March 3, 1801)
3. Thomas Jefferson
   (March 4, 1801–March 3, 1809)
4. James Madison
   (March 4, 1809–March 3, 1817)
5. James Monroe
   (March 4, 1817–March 3, 1825)
6. John Quincy Adams
   (March 4, 1825–March 3, 1829)
7. Andrew Jackson
   (March 4, 1829–March 3, 1837)
8. Martin Van Buren
   (March 4, 1837–March 3, 1841)
9. William Henry Harrison
   (March 6, 1841–April 4, 1841)
10. John Tyler
    (April 6, 1841–March 3, 1845)
11. James K. Polk
    (March 4, 1845–March 3, 1849)
12. Zachary Taylor
    (March 5, 1849–July 9, 1850)
13. Millard Fillmore
    (July 10, 1850–March 3, 1853)
14. Franklin Pierce
    (March 4, 1853–March 3, 1857)
15. James Buchanan
    (March 4, 1857–March 3, 1861)
16. Abraham Lincoln
    (March 4, 1861–April 15, 1865)
17. Andrew Johnson
    (April 15, 1865–March 3, 1869)

18. Ulysses S. Grant
    (March 4, 1869–March 3, 1877)
19. Rutherford B. Hayes
    (March 4, 1877–March 3, 1881)
20. James Garfield
    (March 4, 1881–Sept 19, 1881)
21. Chester Arthur
    (Sept 20, 1881–March 3, 1885)
22. Grover Cleveland
    (March 4, 1885–March 3, 1889)
23. Benjamin Harrison
    (March 4, 1889–March 3, 1893)
24. Grover Cleveland
    (March 4, 1893–March 3, 1897)
25. William McKinley
    (March 4, 1897–
    September 14, 1901)
26. Theodore Roosevelt
    (September 14, 1901–
    March 3, 1909)
27. William Howard Taft
    (March 4, 1909–March 3, 1913)
28. Woodrow Wilson
    (March 4, 1913–March 3, 1921)
29. Warren G. Harding
    (March 4, 1921–August 2, 1923)
30. Calvin Coolidge
    (August 3, 1923–March 3, 1929)
31. Herbert Hoover
    (March 4, 1929–March 3, 1933)
32. Franklin D. Roosevelt
    (March 4, 1933–April 12, 1945)

33. Harry S. Truman
    (April 12, 1945–
    January 20, 1953)
34. Dwight D. Eisenhower
    (January 20, 1953–
    January 20, 1961)
35. John F. Kennedy
    (January 20, 1961–
    November 22, 1963)
36. Lyndon B. Johnson
    (November 22, 1963–
    January 20, 1969)
37. Richard M. Nixon
    (January 20, 1969–
    August 9, 1974)
38. Gerald R. Ford
    (August 9, 1974–
    January 20, 1977)
39. James Earl Carter
    (January 20, 1977–
    January 20, 1981)
40. Ronald Reagan
    (January 20, 1981–
    January 20, 1989)
41. George H. W. Bush
    (January 20, 1989–
    January 20, 1993)
42. William Jefferson Clinton
    (January 20, 1993–
    January 20, 2001)
43. George W. Bush
    (January 20, 2001–)

INDEX

★ ★ ★

<table>
<tr><td>

Agricultural Adjustment Act, 27
agriculture, 20, 21, *25*, 31
Allied Powers, 39, 41, 43, 44–45, 48
Axis Powers, 39, 48

Big Three, 41, *42*, 46, *46*
Black Thursday, 21
Black Tuesday, 22, *22*

Churchill, Winston, 41, *42*, *46*, 48
Civilian Conservation Corps, 27, *28*
Cox, James, 17, *17*

D-Day, 45
Democratic Party, 11, 16, 17,
    23, *44*

Emergency Banking Relief Act,
    27, *27*

Fala (dog), *19*, *50*
Federal Deposit Insurance
    Corporation, 27
"fireside chats," 30–31, *30*
four freedoms, 40
France, 37, *38*, 39, 43, 45
Franklin Delano Roosevelt
    Memorial, *50*

Garner, John N., 23

</td><td>

Germany, 16, 35, 36, 38, 41
Great Britain, 15, 37–38, 39, 41
Great Depression, 6, 22–23,
    23, 25, 28, *32*, 34–35, *34*, 37
Great Plains, *31*
Groton School, 10

Harvard University, 11
Hitler, Adolf, 35, *35*, 38
Hoover, Herbert, 22, *22*
Hoovervilles, *23*
Hundred Days, 28
Hyde Park, New York, 9, *9*, *19*

Italy, 39, 41, 43

Japan, 35–36, 39, 40–41

labor unions, 28, 32
labor strikes, 32, *32*, 42
Lange, Dorothea, *34*

map, *47*
McKinley, William, 11

National Industrial Recovery Act,
    27–28, 33
Nazi Party, 35, *35*, 38
New Deal, 24–25, 31, 34
New York state senate, 14–15, *14*

</td></tr>
</table>

63

Index

Peabody, Endicott, 10
Pearl Harbor, Hawaii, 40–41, *40*
Perkins, Frances, 29, *29*
polio, 6, 18–19

Republican Party, 11, 22, 24, 33
Roaring Twenties, 20–21, *21*
Roosevelt, Anna (daughter), *13, 16*
Roosevelt, Eleanor (wife), 7–8, *8,*
    12–13, 13, 16, 29,
Roosevelt, Franklin Delano,
    7, 8, 10, 11, 13, 15, 16, 17, 18,
    19, 20, 24, 26, 27, 29, 30,
    36, 39, 41, 42, 43, 45, 46, 50
  as assistant secretary of U.S. Navy,
    15–16, *15*
  birth of, 9–10
  childhood of, 10, *10*
  death of, 48, *49*
  education of, 10–11
  as governor of New York, 20, *20*
  health of, 6–7, 17–19
  marriage of, 13
  as New York state senator, 14–15,
    14
  presidential campaigns, 24–25,
    24, 25, 31, 38–39, 44–45, *44*
  vice-presidential campaign, 17, *17*
Roosevelt, James (father), 9–10, *11*

Roosevelt, James (son), *13, 16*
Roosevelt, Sara (mother), 10, *10, 11*
Roosevelt, Theodore "Teddy"
    (cousin), 11–12, *12,* 25

Social Security program, 30
socialism, 32–33
Soviet Union, 37, 41, 43, 47
Spanish-American War, 11
Stalin, Joseph, 41, *42, 46,* 47
Supreme Court, 33–34, *33*

Tennessee Valley Authority, 27
Truman, Harry S., 45, *45*

United Nations, 43, 47
USS *Arizona, 40*

Warm Springs, Georgia, 19, 48
Willkie, Wendell L., 38
Woodin, William, *27*
Works Progress Administration
    (WPA), 29–30
World War I, 16
World War II, 6, 37–38, *37, 38,*
    39–41, *40, 41,* 43, *43,* 44–46

Yalta Summit, 46, *46*

ABOUT THE AUTHOR

Michael Burgan is a freelance writer of books for children and adults. A history graduate of the University of Connecticut, he has written more than thirty fiction and nonfiction children's books for various publishers. For adult audiences, he has written news articles, essays, and plays. Michael Burgan is a recipient of an Edpress Award and belongs to the Society of Children's Book Writers and Illustrators.